Mariano Rivera
Saving Grace

FOREWORD BY JORGE POSADA

INTRODUCTION BY MIKE VACCARO

Fans at Yankee Stadium made it clear who they wanted to see on the mound during the 2004 ALCS against the Boston Red Sox. Rivera saved Games 1 and 2 of the series for the Yankees. (N.Y. Post: Charles Wenzelberg)

This book is available in quantity at special discounts for your group or organization.
For further information, contact:

Triumph Books LLC
814 North Franklin Street
Chicago, Illinois 60610
Phone: (312) 337-0747
www.triumphbooks.com

Printed in U.S.A.
ISBN: 978-1-60078-963-2

Content packaged by Mojo Media, Inc.
Joe Funk: Editor
Jason Hinman: Creative Director

Front and back cover photo by New York Post: Charles Wenzelberg

N.Y. Post: Charles Wenzelberg

CONTENTS

Foreword

By Jorge Posada

When *The Post* asked me to write about Mariano Rivera, the words came easy because of the man I knew in the minor leagues and won World Series titles with. He is a special human being. He understands winning more than anybody. He cares about winning more than anybody. We were brought up the right way when it came to competing in the minor leagues. Mariano completed us. I wouldn't have five rings if Mariano's not on our team. He is that special — and I say it again — he is a special man.

We've all seen how his career has gone, but before he became what he is, you could tell he was different.

I knew something was very special about Mariano in 1995. Something just took off. He was throwing 91, 92 (miles per hour) and all of a sudden he was throwing 96, 97. He was throwing it by people nice and easy with the delivery, the ball just jumping out of his hands.

I remember a no-hitter he threw against the Baltimore affiliate, Rochester. The game was shortened by rain after five innings. He was throwing fastballs by professional hitters. They had guys who were in the big leagues and guys who were future prospects. He was ridiculous, going through them like nothing. I knew Mariano from 1991, but not until 1995 did everything click, and you know the history after that.

You look at his career and it might seem hard to pick out one year as being better than another, but 1999 sticks out for me.

We had a great year in 1998. But what we did in 1999…to be able to win World Series back-to-back! Look at Mariano's numbers (major league-leading 45 saves in 66 appearances; 52 strikeouts in 69 innings pitched) and you realize how ridiculous this guy was going through people. He had a special year in 1998 and a special year in 1997 when he had a tough thing at the end of the year in Cleveland. But look at 1999. I was back there for most of the year and I was blessed to be part of this guy's career.

I've been asked if Mariano were ever out of character when he didn't complete the job, and the only thing out of character was him throwing the ball away at second base (on a Damian Miller bunt attempt in the ninth inning of Game 7 of the 2001 World Series in Arizona). That's the only thing — he was a great fielder.

People talk about Luis Gonzalez and the bases loaded (Gonzalez's ninth-inning single in Game 7 won the Series). I kept saying, 'I knew Mariano was going to get it done.' He is that special. Usually, things don't bother me, but throwing

Mariano Rivera and catcher Jorge Posada shake hands after Rivera closed out Game 1 of the 2009 American League Championship Series. Half of the Yankees' "Core Four," Rivera and Posada were teammates from 1995 to 2011. (N.Y. Post: Charles Wenzelberg)

the ball away at second base hurt.

As for retiring, I think he is ready. He was amazing this year, but it's mentally that you retire. Physically, you can still do it and you can come back, but going through what he has been through, especially last year…he wanted to go out on his own terms and he's doing it. He could do it for another three years easily, but it's more mentally than anything.

I was asked how Yankees fans will remember Mariano, and what they will remember is not only how he pitched on the field, but the way he handled himself off the field.

It's going to be tough for somebody to replace him and put on those shoes. We have five championships because of him. I consider him a friend and I consider him a brother.

— **Jorge Posada**
   August 2013

Above: Two of the Yankees' great relievers, Rivera and Goose Gossage, share a moment during spring training in 2012. Gossage was a four-time all-star and totaled 150 saves for the Yankees between 1978 and 1983. Opposite: Future Hall of Famer Rivera shares a moment with Yankees legends Yogi Berra (left) and Whitey Ford (right) on Opening Day at Yankee Stadium in 2010. (N.Y. Post: Charles Wenzelberg)

Introduction

By Mike Vaccaro

It is easiest to remember Mariano Rivera by his greatness, and by the numbers that have grown to define one of the greatest baseball careers — any position, any era — of all time. It is easiest to know his title as baseball's all-time saves leader and his astonishing 42 postseason saves going into his final season, helped along by an unrelenting string of 1-2-3 ninth innings. You prefer advanced metrics? ERA-plus, which measures every pitcher who ever lived based on 100 being average? Rivera is over 200 for his career, a plateau unreached by any other pitcher who ever lived.

Think about *that* one.

If your memory as a Yankees fan extends to 1997, then Rivera has been in the middle of every celebratory snapshot contained within your mental scrapbook: the 1998 World Series clincher in San Diego; the '99 winner at Yankee Stadium, against the Braves; the 2000 Series, at Shea Stadium, Mike Piazza giving a Rivera cutter a ride, but not far enough. Shane Victorino grounding *another* cutter into the ground, toward second base, the final out of the 2009 World Series. And, perhaps most memorable, Rivera seeking out the mound seconds after Aaron Boone's home run landed in the left-field stands, ending Game 7 of the American League Championship Series against the Red Sox, Rivera collapsing on his office after three extraordinary innings of superb work, perhaps the signature moment of a career stuffed with candidates.

Yes. The successes have been staggering.

But in an odd way, in order to get a full understanding, a complete appreciation, of what Rivera has been in his time and to his sport, you almost have to seek out his rare failures. Because it has been in those moments — some that would have, and have, broken lesser men, lesser talents — when his rare grace, elegance, and eloquence has emerged.

"I give him credit," Rivera said after Game 4 of the 1997 AL Division Series, when Sandy Alomar took him out of Jacobs Field to tie a game the Yankees were four outs away from winning. "It was a good pitch and a better swing. I tip my cap to him."

Some pitchers would be beaten, forever, by a moment like that. Not Rivera. Across the next four years, he was as close to perfect as his imperfect vocation allows. The Yankees won three world championships in a row. And were inches away from winning a fourth straight when Luis Gonzalez broke his bat in the bottom of the 10th inning of Game 7 at Bank One Ballpark in Phoenix, dunking a ball over Derek Jeter's head, ending one of the most inspiring runs of all. And this was Rivera, in the immediate aftermath of that soul-crushing defeat:

"It was a blessing to play in a World Series like this one," he said. "We have had a lot of celebrations in this room. They deserve the celebration they're enjoying now."

Three years later, Rivera had the ball in his hands, Game 4 of the 2004 ALCS in Boston, the Yankees three outs from closing out a sweep. And any fan on either side of the Great Divide remembers, precisely, what happened: A walk to Kevin Millar. A stolen base by pinch-runner Dave Roberts. An RBI single by Bill Mueller — one of the few nemeses of Rivera's career. A tie game. And the start of an avalanche that led to the most improbable reversal in baseball history.

And after that game?

"They are great competitors," Rivera said. "That's why this rivalry is as amazing as it is."

Fans at Yankee Stadium look on in September 2011 as Rivera collects his 38th save of the season against the Baltimore Orioles. (N.Y. Post: Charles Wenzelberg)

Yes, you may say: It is easier for those who know success so well and only dabble in failure to be so gracious, but is it really? The art of closing baseball games is rife with examples of men who tried their hand at the job, failed, and were never the same professionally…and occasionally let those disappointments affect them personally, as well. Closing is an all-encompassing responsibility, the weight of victory constantly on your back.

Nobody has done the job as successfully as Mariano Rivera. Ever.

And nobody has ever handled the other side as well, either.

Ever.

"When you look at his body of work, it's staggering," said Joe Girardi, whose arrival in 1996 as a catcher coincided with Rivera's emergence as the game's preeminent set-up man, a moment in time that was itself a set-up to his shift to all-time greatest closer. Girardi was there for quite a few of his early saves, too. "I mean, the numbers literally make you take a pause, and the memory of him going out there day after day is permanent.

"You say about the very special players that they're once-in-a-generation guys. Well, Mo is once in a lifetime."

And now, his time complete, having gathered mementoes and memories from a lifetime after making his farewell tour around the sport, and cheers from the very fans whose hearts he has fractured time and time again — even in Fenway Park, where you'd sooner see a Kennedy booed as a Yankee cheered.

And it's funny: It seems the world — even those segments most harmed by Rivera's routine excellence through the years — is having a harder

Cornerstone
OF A DYNASTY

Then-Yankees catcher Joe Girardi calms down Mariano Rivera after Rivera gave up a game-tying home run to Oakland's Mark McGwire during the Yankees' home opener in 1997 — Rivera's first season as Yankees closer following the departure of John Wetteland. Despite the blown save, manager Joe Torre never lost confidence in his young stopper. (N.Y. Post: Nury Hernandez)

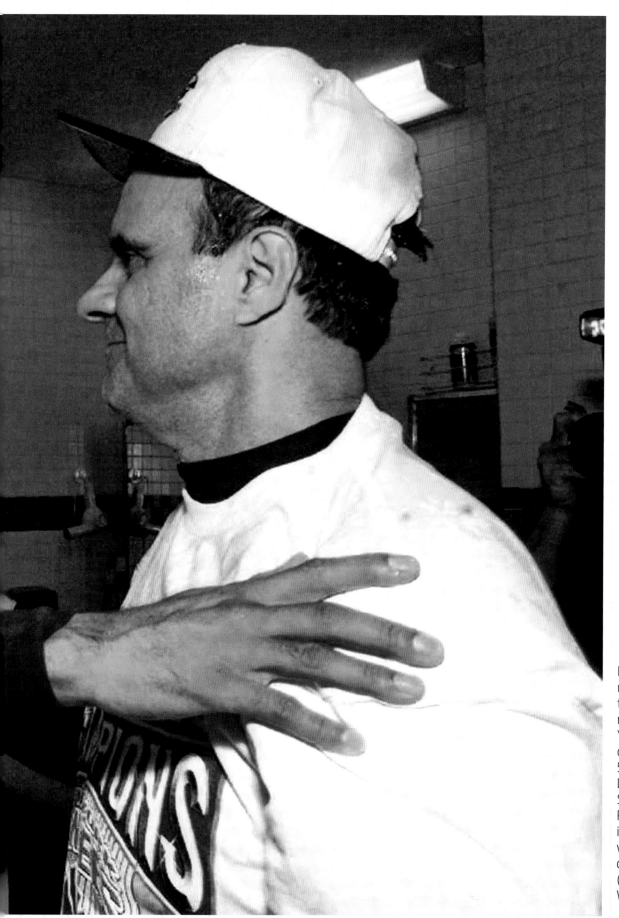

Rivera celebrates with manager Joe Torre in the Yankees locker room following New York's clinching win over Baltimore in Game 5 of the 1996 American League Championship Series. That year, Rivera's first full season in the major leagues, he was the set-up man for closer John Wetteland. (N.Y. Post: Charles Wenzelberg)

The Yankees rush the mound to celebrate after Rivera shut down the Indians in the Yankees' clinching Game 6 of the 1998 ALCS. Rivera pitched 5⅔ scoreless innings over four appearances in the series. (N.Y. Post: Bob Olen)

Rivera celebrates with teammate Derek Jeter following the Yankees' American League-record 112th win in 1998, which topped the mark of 111 by the 1954 Cleveland Indians. Rivera contributed 36 saves and sterling 1.91 ERA to the record-setting season. (N.Y. Post: Charles Wenzelberg)

Rivera First to Finish Line

In Epic Battle of Closing Greats, Mariano Comes Out on Top

October 21, 1998 · By Joel Sherman

Who could save the World? Game 3 of the 1998 World Series came down to a battle of perhaps the two best closers in the majors, San Diego's Trevor Hoffman and the Yankees' Mariano Rivera. Both were asked to pitch more than their normal one inning. Just Rivera prospered. This October, no one saved like Rivera.

Rivera recorded the final five outs for the Yankees, ending the game by striking out Andy Sheets with runners at first and third to cement the Yankees' 5-4 triumph over the Padres.

The Yankees had the lead because Hoffman failed to hold a 3-2 edge he was handed in the eighth inning. The Padres stalwart permitted a three-run homer to Scott Brosius to put the Yankees ahead 5-3.

"It feels good to me," Rivera said when asked if there were anything special to doing his job when his counterpart did not. "But I was just prepared to pitch. Even if he gives up 10 runs, I have to do my job."

Rivera was the Yankees' most dominating player that postseason. Opponents came into Game 3 1-for-29 against the Yankees closer. But San Diego matched the total immediately.

Ramiro Mendoza had allowed a one-out double to Quilvio Veras in the eighth with the Yanks ahead 5-3. Torre brought in Rivera, who surrendered a single to Tony Gwynn. Greg Vaughn followed with a long sacrifice fly to draw San Diego within a run. But Rivera struck out Ken Caminiti to end the inning.

In the ninth, Rivera got two quick outs before consecutive singles to Carlos Hernandez and Mark Sweeney put the tying run 90 feet away and the winning run at first. But Rivera punched his trademark high fastball by Sheets on a 1-2 count and the Yankees celebrated a three-games-to-none lead.

Part of the reason the Yanks were in this post season was the all-but-flawless work of Rivera. By the end of Game 3, the righty had 12 scoreless innings on the postseason, the most by any reliever since St. Louis' Ken Dayley produced the same amount in 1985.

"I feel great," Rivera said. "I feel confident and when you feel confident you feel as if you can go on forever." ∎

Rivera and catcher Joe Girardi celebrate on the mound after the Yankees topped the San Diego Padres in Game 4 to complete a sweep of the 1998 World Series. Rivera totaled three saves in the series. (N.Y. Post: Charles Wenzelberg)

The image of teammates mobbing Mariano Rivera on the mound became synonymous with the Yankees' success in the late 1990s. Here the Yankees celebrate after Game 3 of the 1998 World Series, when Rivera out-pitched Trevor Hoffman in a late-game battle between the best two closers in baseball history. (AP Images)

Rewriting THE RECORD BOOKS

Rivera looks forward to another successful campaign during spring training in 2009. The legendary closer added a fifth World Series ring to his résumé that season. (N.Y. Post: Charles Wenzelberg)

Old Faithful

Mariano Rivera on God, Family, and the N.Y. Yankees

September 21, 2011 · By George A. King III

George A. King III, The Post's Yankees beat writer since 1997, sat down with Mariano Rivera in September 2011 at Rogers Centre in Toronto and chatted with the saves king about his incredible career, faith, family and much more.

New York Post: At what age did you realize you wanted to be a baseball player?

Mariano Rivera: This is a funny thing because I always wanted to be a professional player and play for the New York Yankees but I wasn't pursuing being a professional. God permitted it to happen. I was 20 years old and pitching and the Yankees came and signed me. Right when I put my feet on the steps at the airport in Tampa, I realized, "You know what, this is for real." I had never left my country (Panama) before. I said, "You know what. If I am going to be here and leave my country and my family and everybody I left behind, I am going to be the best. That was the day I realized I wanted to give it the best shot that I could."

NYP: You come to Tampa and had no idea it was going to go this way. Were you homesick?

MR: The first week I was miserable, but everything I do I give my best. Everything starts with God in my career and it will finish with God.

NYP: How long has God been a big part of your life?

MR: Since I was 20, 21. As an athlete, you know your abilities and I knew my abilities weren't enough for me to be in the big leagues, never mind what I have accomplished. God took those abilities and made me better.

NYP: Is 600 just a number or is it a testament to longevity and not having serious injuries? Or is it, "This is what my career has become?"

MR: The blessing of the Lord is No. 1 and then you have the longevity. Then you have to throw in resting and taking care of yourself. There is no way, if you don't take care of yourself, you can expect to play 10 years. It's a combination of everything."

NYP: Reggie Jackson said watching Mariano Rivera on the mound looks like death on the cover of GQ. It's very serious and very calm. Where does that come from?

A humble superstar, Rivera credits God and his teammates for his many accomplishments. (N.Y. Post: Charles Wenzelberg)

MR: Ever since I was a little kid, I was competitive. When I am on the mound, it is competition and I have to make it happen. Again, I have to mention the Lord because everything around me begins with the Lord. The Lord's blessing has gotten me here for all these years. The Lord takes control of everything.

NYP: You raced to the Yankee Stadium mound and kissed the rubber after Aaron Boone's 2003 ALCS-winning home run. For a guy who doesn't show much emotion, what caused that?

MR: It was kind of personal. When I saw Boone hit that home run, my only thing was going to the place that I feel connected to. I didn't care who saw me or if they laughed, I didn't care about it. I wanted to thank the Lord. He permitted it to happen.

NYP: You have had so much success, World Series rings, All-Star Games and 600 saves. What has the sacrifice been to your family?

MR: Without the support of my family — and even though they are Christians and have to have blessings, you still have to have the support of your family — I don't see how I would have accomplished any of this. My family has played a big, big, big role.

NYP: When you arrived in spring training in February, you talked about how every year it gets harder to leave your family in Westchester. Next year, you will be older. How tough will that be?

MR: Next year will be even tougher, but I have been blessed because my family has supported me all the way. Moving on, they know the end of my career is coming soon.

NYP: When is the end of your career?

MR: I have another year on the contract. After that I don't know what is going to happen. I will make a decision soon, even before next season is over.

NYP: Do you take games home with you? Big wins, killer losses?

MR: When I don't do the job, there is a tendency for it to bother me on the way home, but it goes away because I don't want to take that home.

NYP: Even 2001 in Phoenix?

MR: No, because I did everything in my power to help us. That's my thing, I check myself. If I put all the effort and I know 100 percent that I did that, then I am OK.

NYP: What do you feel like when you hear Mariano Rivera is the best closer ever, perhaps the best pitcher ever?

MR: I don't let those things get to my mind. I don't feel like that. I am not. I am just a guy who is blessed with a tremendous team, a tremendous gift from the Lord and the support of my wife and family.

NYP: Has your family ever asked you about all the summers you have missed being with them?

MR: Yes, my family has approached me on that. We talk as a family and come to an agreement but this is what I love to do and what I know to do. I just want to make sure when I leave this game, I don't want to have any regrets. We talk about it and we will come to a decision: Continue or stop?

NYP: What did Joe Torre making you the closer in 1997, even though you had very little experience doing that, feel like?

MR: What made that happen was the 1996 season. I remember at the beginning of the year I was a long reliever. But everything fell into place. As a long reliever, it is hard for the

During the 2010 American League Championship Series, Mariano Rivera takes the field at Yankee Stadium as part of pregame introductions. When No. 42 was retired across the major leagues in 1997 in honor of Jackie Robinson, players currently wearing the number were allowed to continue wearing it. Rivera's retirement marks the last active player to wear No. 42. (N.Y. Post: Charles Wenzelberg)

manager to see you. Everything that has happened around me, God permitted. The more I pitched as a long reliever, I pitched good. That allowed me to become the set-up man. That was the key.

NYP: Did you have doubt that you could close games?

MR: The first month as a closer was hard. I was trying so hard to do the job that it was impossible for me to do it. I remember Joe calling me into his office and he said, "It doesn't matter what happens, you will be my closer." I mean you know and I know and everybody knows this, if I didn't do my job, I wouldn't be the closer. But I took those words as so encouraging that it was different. I had 43 saves that year.

NYP: You left Panama at 20 and have been in New York a long time. Are you a New Yorker?

MR: I have to be honest, I wouldn't say I am a New Yorker. I will always be a Panamanian. My roots and my family are in Panama. But I consider myself a New Yorker because New York has given me so many opportunities. The people have taken me as one of them. I have been blessed that the city of New York has provided so much for (me) but I can't change my roots.

NYP: Whenever you are done, what are you going to do?

MR: We have a lot of jobs to do with the church. That takes a lot from you. You have to want to do that and I want to do that.

NYP: Are you a demanding parent?

MR: I would say yes in all the ways. I demand my kids be respectful, responsible and grateful. And they have to love the Lord with all their hearts. I am not a father who wants to give his kids everything. They have to earn it. ∎

A humble player who was known for being accommodating to fans, Rivera signs autographs during spring training in 2012. (N.Y. Post: Charles Wenzelberg)

Unbeatable King of Playoffs

Dominant Closer Earns MVP Honors with Win and Two Saves

October 28, 1999 · By Kevin Kernan

There was a happy ending to a week in which the Latino community was robbed by Major League Baseball by having its icon, Roberto Clemente, overlooked on the All-Century team. As the Yankees completed their 1999 World Series sweep of the Atlanta Braves, a new hero emerged for another generation to worship. And he was the same kind of caring individual as the great Clemente.

Mariano Rivera ascended to the throne as the best reliever in the majors and the greatest ERA postseason pitcher of them all. Yankees fans can point to a long list of Yankees heroes following the team's third championship in four seasons, but they don't dare overlook the presence of Rivera, who earned Series MVP honors. He was the Yankees' silent killer. And he was a weapon in this World Series that the Braves could not match, not even with John Rocker. And Rivera didn't smash any Corvettes.

"I was the guy throwing the last pitch," Rivera said, "and it felt tremendous."

It seems he was always the guy throwing the last pitch for the greatest team in baseball, the team of the decade, a team that to that point had won three World Series Championships in four years, including back-to-back titles.

"It's impossible to repeat those kind of numbers," Rivera said of the Yankees' dominant 1998 team after he recorded the last out of the Yankees' clinching 4-1 victory over the Braves to clinch the 1999 Series at the Stadium. "But we won the American League. We won the Division. We were the best team in the American League. We won the World Series. We swept Atlanta, one of the best teams. To me, it means a lot to win back-to-back championships. And I did my little job."

It's not little.

Rivera is the best postseason weapon ever. And I don't need a panel of baseball experts to tell me that. He picked up his second save of the Series to go along with one victory, by pitching another 1⅓ innings of shutout baseball in Game 4. With the tying runs on base in the eighth, he got the Braves' best hitter, Chipper Jones, to bounce to second for the final out of the inning.

Then he worked another silent ninth. His career postseason ERA stood at 0.38 (two earned runs in 47⅓ innings). He pitched 4 scoreless innings with a win and two saves in three appearances in the 1999 World Series. He pitched 12⅓ scoreless innings with

Rivera and catcher Jorge Posada celebrate on the mound after Rivera closed out the Yankees' clinching Game 4 win over the Atlanta Braves in the 1999 World Series. Rivera pitched 4⅔ scoreless innings with a win and two saves to earn series MVP honors. (AP Images)

two wins and six saves in eight appearances in the 1999 postseason. He fired 13⅓ scoreless innings in the 1998 postseason and had not allowed a run in his last 25⅔ innings in postseason play over 18 outings, with two wins and 12 saves in that span. His last postseason run allowed was Sandy Alomar's home run in the 1997 playoffs. His last World Series run came in Game 3, 1996, against the Braves. Rivera is a cut-fastball genius.

The previous low postseason ERA mark belonged to Harry Brecheen of the old St. Louis Browns, 0.83, three earned runs in 32⅔ innings, but those numbers were put up in the war years of 1943 and '44. Brecheen also pitched in the 1946 World Series. The other pitcher to post a phenomenal World Series ERA was a guy named Babe Ruth, who posted an ERA of 0.87 with the Red Sox in the 1916 and 1918 World Series.

Nothing bothers Rivera, not even the streak.

"I just don't even think about it," he said before the game. "I go to the mound and just try to do my job and don't think about the runs, you know, I'm in a spot. I can't afford to give up any runs, so I don't think about it."

It's all about the challenge of the save, Rivera said. "I believe in the challenge. I love the challenge. I love to be in that situation where, I guess, that's my motivation."

Rivera started as a setup man and learned much under John Wetteland, whom he is quick to credit for his success. "The setup man has a net," Rivera said. "The closer doesn't have nothing, so he falls, I mean he's dead."

Of Wetteland, he said, "John was my teacher. He was my friend at the time. He never gave up. I follow him close and see what he was doing. I take that approach."

Wetteland saved all four Yankees wins in the '96 Series to earn MVP honors. The Yankees lost Wetteland and many thought he never could be replaced. Instead they had an even more fearsome weapon. The circle is complete. ■

Rivera warms up before entering Game 4 of the 1999 World Series against the Braves. Rivera earned his third World Series ring as the Yankees won their second consecutive championship. (AP Images)

Rivera's Best, Case Closed

Mo Puts Yankees Over the Top

October 27, 2000 · By Joel Sherman

At 5:20 p.m. before Game 5 of the 2000 World Series, "Enter Sandman" by Metallica cranked through Shea Stadium and Mets players hit line drives to all fields. How nice for the Mets that this was Shea and the guy throwing batting practice was bullpen catcher Dave Racaniello.

Normally, "Enter Sandman" is a funeral dirge for hitters because it is the song that brings Mariano Rivera to the mound. And in October, batters would rather hear that bats will be made of paper next year than hear Rivera's theme. Because Halloween does not close October as well as Rivera does.

"They have a lot of great players," Mets manager Bobby Valentine said of the Yankees. "But as far as value, he is in another category."

As midnight came, the Mets were not as fortunate as they had been in late afternoon. Rivera was on his game, and in a matchup from baseball heaven he got Mike Piazza to fly to deep center as the tying run to seal the Yankees' World Series-clinching 4-2 triumph over the Mets. For the third straight year, Rivera

threw the last pitch of a baseball season. This time, it was strong enough to stop a Subway.

The Yankees had exceptional starting pitching; so did the Braves and Mets. The Yankees had a good defense, but not as good as Cleveland or San Francisco. The Yankees had an effective, veteran lineup, but the White Sox and A's had orders that posed at least as much a threat.

At this time of year, the Yankees separate themselves from all other teams for one reason — a 30-year-old cutter-throwing dynamo.

"If you had to delineate the one reason the Yankees win, he is the most unique, distinct reason," Indians assistant general manager Mark Shapiro said. "Other teams match up with the Yankees in other areas, but Rivera is the most unique component. No other club has that."

In 1996, Rivera was the Yankees' best pitcher as the set-up man for John Wetteland, and for the 1998, 1999, and 2000 championship seasons, he has been their most important pitcher.

With him, the Yankees play October games

Rivera and teammates celebrate at Shea Stadium after the Yankees closer retired the Mets' Mike Piazza to complete the Yankees' third consecutive World Series title. (N.Y. Post: Charles Wenzelberg)

"No one else throws a 94 mph cutter, It's like bird-watching in a foreign land. You can't understand it."
—Mets manager Bobby Valentine

backward. If they lead after seven innings, they win. So Joe Torre is always pushing to gain the lead by then and opposing managers are doing everything to avoid an eighth-inning deficit. The Yankees scored twice in the top of the ninth in Game 5 and since that got Rivera to warm up, the 2000 baseball season was over.

"He's not an illusion, he's the real deal," Valentine said of Rivera. "[To have a great closer] is what gives a team confidence. It's what gives a team wins. And he's the best one at it, so they have a little more than other teams at the end of games."

Since 1996, Torre has operated with a weapon no other team can deploy, what has gone from an October surprise to a fall classic. Since 1996, Rivera has dominated the postseason.

In Game 5, he permitted a one-out walk to Benny Agbayani in the ninth before getting Edgardo Alfonzo to fly to right and Piazza to end the season.

Since Torre took over as manager, opponents are hitting .178 off Rivera with a .221 on-base percentage and a feeble .243 slugging percentage. He has allowed a .150 batting average with runners in scoring position. He has never allowed two hits with runners in scoring position in any of his 41 postseason games.

But the brilliance of Rivera is best understood in comparisons to his contemporaries. Mark Wohlers saved 39 games in the 1996 season, but not the World Series Game 4 against the Yankees he absolutely had to.

Trevor Hoffman saved 53 games in 1998, but not the World Series Game 3 against the Yankees he absolutely had to. Armando Benitez saved 41 games in 2000, but not the World Series Game 1 against the Yankees he absolutely had to. So Atlanta lost to the Yankees in 1996, San Diego to the Yankees in 1998 and the Mets lost in 2000.

Overall, Rivera is 4-0 in the postseason with an 0.71 ERA. He has converted 19 of 20 saves. The lone failure came in Game 4 of the 1997 Division Series, when Sandy Alomar homered off him, and the Yankees ultimately were eliminated. Rivera responded by running off his next 18 postseason save tries, including the 2000 World Series clincher.

Jay Payton hit a two-run homer off Rivera in the ninth inning of the Yankees' 6-5, Game 2 victory. However, when he had to, Rivera struck out Kurt Abbott to close that game. In Game 4, with a one-run margin of error, Rivera retired six of the seven batters he faced as he continued to give Torre a two-inning close option. Last night, he authored yet another shutout inning.

Valentine said Rivera threw his hitters almost exclusively cutters. The hitters knew it was coming, but so what?

"No one else throws a 94 mph cutter," Valentine said. "It's like bird-watching in a foreign land. You can't understand it."

Rivera is a strange bird indeed, one that soars higher and higher in October, one strong enough to carry an entire team on a single wing. A savior to a champion again. ■

Mariano Rivera savors the atmosphere in Yankee Stadium during warm-ups before Game 1 of the 2000 World Series between the Mets and Yankees. (N.Y. Post: Nury Hernandez)

Mo Makes His Mark

Rivera's 47th Save Breaks Righetti's Club Record

September 24, 2001 · By George King

The hurt from two nights earlier had been tossed into the Inner Harbor waters. In Mariano Rivera's head the flush job against the Orioles was already out to sea.

Now, after the Yankees battled back to take a one-run lead in extra innings, Joe Torre did what he had done for the previous five seasons in a save situation: He went to Mo.

And was rewarded with a 5-4, 10-inning win in front of a Camden Yards crowd of 446,071.

The victory snapped a three-game losing streak, reduced the Yankees' magic number to two to clinch the AL East and kept them 3½ games ahead of the Indians in the race for the second-best record in the AL and the home-field advantage in the first round of the playoffs.

Rivera, who was bruised two nights earlier when his fastball was straight as a string, was dominating. He got Jeff Conine on a grounder to the mound, Chris Richard on a grounder to first and notched his club-record 47th save by fanning Cal Ripken.

"It's going to be special," Rivera said of the ball he took from his record-setting save that broke Dave Righetti's single-season club record, set in 1986.

Since taking over for John Wetteland as the Yankees' closer at the start of 1997, Rivera has been special.

For seven innings, it appeared Rivera wasn't going to get a chance to surpass Righetti since the Yankees were trailing, 4-1, going to the eighth. But Nick Johnson, who homered in the sixth, drove a two-run double to left and suddenly the Yankees had a chance to avoid being swept by the putrid Orioles.

Bernie Williams' sacrifice fly tied the score, 4-4, in the ninth and Williams drew a bases-loaded walk from John Parrish in the 10th to give Rivera a 5-4 lead.

Two nights earlier Rivera also had a one-run lead and four batters later he had a blown save and a loss. Yet, when he went to work this night, the blown save may have well been another century.

"Those games are tough," Rivera said. "But I learned a long time ago to forget them. I have to put them behind me."

Closing for five years, it's somewhat surprising that Rivera didn't break Righetti's record sooner.

"I don't know why, I have had a lot of opportunities and I have been healthy," Rivera said.

Williams, who struggled since play resumed following the Sept. 11 terrorist attacks, gave Rivera his latest chance.

"It was a 3-2 slider, up and away and very tough to lay off," Williams said of his game-winning walk. "It certainly wasn't pretty but I will take it." ■

Rivera accepts congratulations from Yankees manager Joe Torre after Rivera saved the Yankees' 5-4 win at Baltimore on September 23, 2001. The save was Rivera's 47th of the season, breaking the club mark held by Dave Righetti. (Getty Images)

First Yankee to 50

Rivera Hits Historic Save Mark

October 8, 2001 · By George King

After becoming the sixth pitcher to post 50 saves, Mariano Rivera's magic number was 11.

"I do, but I don't show those things," Rivera said when asked if 50 saves were a big accomplishment. "Especially when the focus is on getting 11 wins, those are the big ones."

Of course, in order for the Yankees to cop a fourth straight World Series title, they need to win 11 postseason games.

"It's good, but I will go for these games coming up," Rivera said.

Rivera joined Bobby Thigpen (57), Trevor Hoffman (53), Randy Myers (53), Rod Beck (51) and Dennis Eckersley (51) in the 50-Save Club but he didn't stuff the ball into his bag.

Instead, the ball went to Luis Sojo.

"Louie asked me for the ball before the game," Rivera said of his close friend who is in grave danger of not making the postseason roster. "He is trying to retire and it's something nice."

"I have been telling you guys this is my last year," said the 2010 World Series hero. "Hopefully, there will be more games so I can go home happy." ■

The 2001 season marked several historical accomplishments for Rivera. He topped Dave Righetti's single-season club record for saves became the first Yankee to eclipse 50 saves in a season. Rivera's success continued in the playoffs. Here he accepts the embrace of a teammate following the Yankees' clinching win over the Oakland A's in Game 5 of the ALDS. (N.Y. Post: Charles Wenzelberg)

A teammate from 1995 to 2011, catcher Jorge Posada was on the receiving end of many of Rivera's greatest accomplishments on the mound. Here the pitcher and catcher shake hands following a May 2003 Yankees win. (N.Y. Post: Nury Hernandez)

Yankees Save King

"Reachable" Rivera Gets 225th Save

May 10, 2002 · By George King

Mariano Rivera's saves aren't as dominant as they have been across a career that could carry him into the Hall of Fame. Hitters are more aggressive and Devil Rays manager Hal McRae said the Yankees closer looked "reachable."

Maybe if he weren't facing the worst team in baseball that is on a 14-game bender, Rivera may have paid a price for not being razor sharp.

But it was the Devil Rays and that meant Rivera worked out of an eighth-inning jam and retired three of the four batters in the ninth for the save in the Yankees' 3-1 win.

It was Rivera's 10th save in 12 chances in 2002 and the 225th of his career, which set the Yankees record.

While Rivera downplayed passing Dave Righetti in Yankees history, Joe Torre gushed about the best closer in baseball. "Rivera deserves every record he can get, he is the best I have ever seen," Torre said.

Rivera smiled at Torre's message. "That's a good compliment but I don't live on that," he said. "I lived on what I do now. I respect Joe because he is like a father but I have to do my job." ∎

Even passing Dave Righetti on the all-time saves list in the Yankees' record book couldn't shake Rivera's calm, humble demeanor. (AP Photo/Winslow Townson)

Rivera Mo's 'Em Down

Closer Named ALCS MVP

October 17, 2003 · By Lenn Robbins

After Mike Mussina stopped the bleeding in Game 7 of the ALCS with a dazzling relief performance and the Yankees rallied for an overwhelming 6-5 win over the Red Sox in 11 innings, the Moose had enough of relieving.

"Remind me, I want to be a starter," Mussina said to Joe Torre.

Mussina can remain a starter because Mariano Rivera proved once again he is greatest closer in baseball, maybe the greatest ever. Rivera suffocated the Red Sox for three innings until Aaron Boone smacked a walk-off home run to send the Yankees to the World Series.

"I was thinking, 'We have to get this game,'" said Rivera, who was the named the MVP of the series. "I have to do my best and get a chance to win, give him [Boone] a chance to hit that home run. I'm proud of my teammates. They did tremendous. I mean, it was outstanding."

No one was more outstanding in the series than Rivera. He worked two innings to save Game 5. He worked two innings to save Game 3. He worked one inning to save Game 2.

In Game 7, the 6-foot-2, 185-pounder showed he has a strength and endurance that belies his stature. Rivera threw 48 pitches; 33 were strikes. With each batter he strangled the hope out of the Red Sox.

"The guy is superhuman," said slugger Jason Giambi. "I mean, he's a cartoon. You can't destroy him. If he gets tired, he doesn't show it. He just goes out there and throws, throws, throws. I've never seen anything like it."

At the end of the day, the difference between the Yankees and every other team in baseball is Rivera. Before the 2003 season, Boston manager Grady Little joked that he still didn't know who was his closer.

The Yankees have known all along who theirs is. Rivera was the MVP in the 1999 World Series. He was almost untouchable in the ALCS, striking out six, walking none and allowing just one earned run and five hits in eight innings.

Rivera hadn't gone three innings since September 1996 and this was his longest outing since he went 2⅔ innings on April 19, 2000.

"There's obviously no one else I'd rather have the ball at the end of the game than Mo," said instant hero Boone.

"I'm glad you said that," joked Rivera. ∎

Teammates carry Rivera off the field after the Yankees' epic 11-inning win over the Boston Red Sox in Game 7 of the 2003 ALCS. Rivera was named series MVP, allowing just one run and five hits in eight innings. (N.Y. Post: Charles Wenzelberg)

Rivera and fellow Yankees hurler Orlando "El Duque" Hernandez look on during the 2000 World Series against the Mets. The two right-handers were integral parts to the Yankees' third consecutive championship. (N.Y. Post: Charles Wenzelberg)

To the
MOUNTAINTOP

Mariano Rivera pops a bottle of champagne in the clubhouse after the Yankees clinched the American League East in 2006. Rivera posted 34 saves and a 1.80 ERA during the regular season. (N.Y. Post: Charles Wenzelberg)

Heading Home

Rivera: Panama Is Where My Heart Is

May 11, 2010 · By Michael Starr

Derek Jeter and Alex Rodriguez live large — on and off the field at Yankee Stadium. But the other immortal Yankee, Mariano Rivera — arguably the best relief pitcher who ever lived and the closest thing to a unanimous Hall of Famer playing the game — is a still a mystery to most people.

He is from Panama — a country better known for producing jockeys than baseball players — and, in a 2010 ESPN profile, Mo took American TV cameras into the world he came from.

Before the season started, ESPN reporter Tom Rinaldi traveled with Rivera to his hometown of Puerto Caimito, Panama, where the pitcher was born in poverty and still owns a home — now as one of the richest and probably most famous people in the country.

"This is my town, this is where my heart is," he says, driving through Puerto Caimito. "It's a poor town with poor people…who either have a little bit or have none at all."

Rivera, who was signed as a 19-year-old — and arrived in the U.S. speaking no English — goes back to the crude, oceanfront ballfield where he learned to play ball.

You had to know how to control the bat, he explains, and hit the ball "straight up" over second base.

Anything else would land in the ocean.

Rivera and his wife, Clara, whom he has known since kindergarten, hand out backpacks with school supplies to local children (in Panama, Rivera is famous for his charity work).

He tells how he used to work with his father, a boat captain — and the life that he was supposed to lead before finding baseball. Turns out, he came close to perishing when their boat sank far offshore in the Pacific.

"It was hard work, dangerous, and lot of people have lost arms, legs, lives," the soft-spoken Rivera says of his boating days, describing how the boat sank because of "too many fish" and a malfunctioning water pump.

"We were in the open seas, thank God next to an island and able to stop there and save ourselves," he says of his near-death experience.

The 11-minute profile highlighted Rivera's requisite baseball stats, World Series records and clips of him in action.

"My confidence never changed because I know who I trust and I know who I am," Rivera says.

"My imprint has to be that I did everything within my power to help others to do the right thing, for the New York Yankees, my teammates, my family…and that alone, I'll be happy with that." ■

Mariano Rivera and his wife, Clara, wave to fans during the 2008 All-Star Game parade. The Riveras, who met in kindergarten, are known for their charity work in both Panama and the United States. (N.Y. Post: Chad Rachman)

Rivera shares fist-bumps with coaches and teammates following a save against Cleveland in July 2005. The Yankees closer racked up 43 saves that season. (N.Y. Post: Charles Wenzelberg)

Rivera the Restaurateur

Mo Goes from Closer to Setup Man at Steak Eatery with Pal

October 27, 2006 · By Kevin Kernan

The young pitcher didn't know anyone in New York. He didn't even know how to get to Yankee Stadium.

Joe Fosina, who has handled Yankee uniform alterations and reconditioning of equipment since the 1970s, lived in the same area where the pitcher was going to stay, so a club official asked Joe to drop him off that night in 1995. Fosina did and gave the pitcher his phone number. He said if he needed anything, call.

The next day, Fosina's phone rang. His wife, Mickie, picked up. On the other end was the young pitcher, who was just starting to learn English. "Mr. Joe…Stadium."

Enter Sandman. Mariano Rivera needed a ride to Yankee Stadium.

"God put Joe Fosina in my life to help me out," Rivera said 413 saves later, "I didn't even know how to get to the Stadium. So I called Joe."

From that brief conversation, an amazing family friendship has developed. Rivera essentially became Fosina's sixth son. There was John, Gary, Danny, Michael, Kenny — and now Mariano. "I can call him at 1 or 2 o'clock in the morning, and he is there for me," Rivera says of Fosina. The kid from Panama and the family from New Rochelle bonded, so much so that in 1999 Joe and Mickie went to Panama. Mickie even got the chance to push the button to open the locks of the Panama Canal.

"Mariano took my camera and took the video of me opening the canal," Mickie says. "He is just a beautiful person, and you can't believe how big he is down there," adding that Rivera is so famous, he is even waved through tollbooths. "Yet, when we get to the hotel, Mariano opens up the hatch on the car and he carries our luggage into the hotel."

"That's me," Rivera offers with a smile.

"We always get together," Rivera says of his family and the Fosinas. "Her sons are all great guys. You want your family to be like that. The joy that I see in that family is wonderful. It's a perfect example of what a family should be."

Every Fourth of July when the Yankees were home, Rivera, his wife, Clara, and their children would go to a barbecue at the Fosina home. Gary Fosina, a chef, would do the cooking. The food was terrific, so good that Fosina became the head chef at Mo's New York Grill, a restaurant that opened in July 2006 in New Rochelle. Rivera partnered with the Fosina family in the upscale steakhouse.

Mariano Rivera poses with head chef Gary Fosina (right) and chef John Hays at Mo's New York Grill in 2006. (Photo by Anthony J. Causi)

Rivera is a proud man, and his name was on the restaurant and throughout the mahogany-theme dining room. Rivera made it clear to Gary that he wanted a classy yet comfortable restaurant, a place that exemplified what he is on the mound. Rivera offered some key design features: the arched hallway, the crown molding and a gorgeous corner fish tank, a tribute to his fisherman father.

The restaurant business is a tough business. Rivera knew his name would get people in the door, but they would have to want to come back because of the job done by Gary Fosina. Fosina, 44, was Mariano's closer in this deal.

"Gary and the whole staff have done a tremendous job," Rivera says, noting Donald Trump, Joe Torre and Brian Cashman have eaten at the restaurant and all offered compliments. On a Wednesday night, there was a great crowd, and Rivera is not shy about seeking out instant reviews from customers.

"We want the public to enjoy this place, feel like they are home and have a nice time," Rivera explained. "I love to come here and talk to people and see how they respond. I want feedback — tell me the truth about the restaurant and what they would want to see improved. It's no different than pitching."

Rivera does not take his gifts for granted. He has reached out to help others, building a church in Panama and quietly doing many good deeds to help people here and back home.

"I have received a lot, and I have a grateful heart," Rivera explains. "I think it's good to give back."

Joe Fosina is seated at the table and nods. He thinks back to that first drive with Mariano, how proudly Rivera has worn the Pinstripes and what No. 42 means to the Yankees and their fans. He smiles and promises there is one more drive he will make with Mariano.

"I've told him," Fosina says, "we'll be driving up to Cooperstown in about eight years." ∎

Mariano Rivera shares a moment with longtime friends and business partners Joe Fosina (left) and Gary Fosina (right) at Mo's New York Grill in New Rochelle, New York. Joe Fosina, who handled Yankees uniform alterations and reconditioning for decades, drove Rivera to Yankee Stadium after the young pitcher reached the major leagues in 1995. (Photo by Anthony J. Causi)

Rivera's Saving Grace

Mariano Notches No. 300

May 29, 2004 · By Michael Morrissey

Minutes after Mariano Rivera closed out the Yankees' 7-5 victory over Tampa Bay, Joe Torre interrupted him in the shower to give him the umpire's lineup cards from his 300th career save.

Rivera, washing off the sweat that yielded his milestone, doesn't have many souvenirs from his Hall-of-Fame bound career. It's simply not his style to get caught up in himself — a major reason for his success.

"He said, 'Put it on the chair,' without any emotion whatsoever," Torre said.

On a night the Bombers couldn't quite score double figures or break away from the pesky Devil Rays, the unflappable Rivera was there to slam the door shut for his team's fifth straight victory.

Ruben Sierra, Gary Sheffield, Hideki Matsui and Derek Jeter homered to account for all of the runs as the offensive onslaught continued. Nevertheless, this one will be remembered because their teammate became the 17th reliever — and first Yankee — to reach the 300-save club.

Rivera, who began closing games for the Yankees in 1997, was clearly proud of the feat. However, he was unwilling to dwell too long on its significance.

"Personally, it's OK, it's good," he said at one point. "It's nice to have it. There are other things to win…

"Don't get me wrong — it's something nice I appreciate. One day I will think about [being inducted into] the Hall of Fame."

Rivera explained that the accomplishment pales in comparison to the four world championships he has been a part of — one as a setup man and three as a closer.

His teammates, new and old, made up for Rivera's modesty.

"Anybody who knows Mo knows he is probably the most consistent closer there's ever been," Sheffield said.

"We put everything in his hands," Bernie Williams added. "He's been able to deliver. I think it's remarkable."

Sheffield's tie-breaking three-run jack with one out in the fifth was the big blow, but every dinger mattered as the Yankees improved to 7-3 on their longest road trip of the season — a 12-game span that has become a Trail of Destruction. They remain

Joe Torre congratulates Rivera after the closer's 300th career save. Torre managed the Yankees from 1996 to 2007, winning four World Series. (AP Images)

"Anybody who knows Mo knows he is probably the most consistent closer there's ever been."

—Yankees outfielder Gary Sheffield

a half-game behind the Red Sox.

With two outs in the fourth, Sierra sparked the offense. He smashed a 3-and-0 cripple pitch by starter Doug Waechter halfway up the right-field stands for a game-tying two-run homer.

Jeter, on an 11-for-25 five-game tear, opened the fifth by legging out a double to the left-field corner. With one out, Waechter fell behind Alex Rodriguez 3-and-0 before issuing an intentional walk. Sheffield then crushed a 1-and-0 fastball into the seats in left for his fifth homer.

Two batters later, Matsui hit a solo homer to make it 6-2. But the Devil Rays rallied off Javier Vazquez and Paul Quantrill in the seventh before Tom Gordon escaped.

Gordon loaded the bases with one out and allowed a fielder's choice groundout that put Tampa Bay within 6-5. But he whiffed Robert Fick to end the seventh and stranded the tying run on second in the eighth.

In the ninth, Jeter hit a solo shot to right-center to give some breathing room to Rivera, who allowed a leadoff single to Aubrey Huff before retiring the next three men to reach the record books.

"It's pretty impressive," said Jeter, one of his oldest teammates. "He's the best." ■

Rivera accepts congratulations from catcher Jorge Posada after closing out Tampa Bay to reach 300 career saves on May 28, 2004. (AP Images)

Rivera of Dreams

Closer Gets Save No. 400

July 17, 2006 · By Michael Morrissey

Mariano Rivera can't recall anything about his first career save on May 17, 1996, the memories having receded like his hairline over the years.

One thing remained constant through 10 seasons as Yankees closer, however. A dominance unparalleled in baseball. Never was that clearer than when Rivera was called upon to record six outs for his 400th career save against the second-best team in the American League.

The 36-year-old reliever tossed double-play balls in both the eighth and ninth, culminating an impressive, confidence-building sweep of the wild-card leading White Sox with a 6-4 victory.

"It was special," Rivera said. "They made me work for this one. It's amazing. Amazing. I would never even think about that."

Jason Giambi called Rivera "the most dominating closer this game has ever seen." He stood as the all-time AL save leader and only trailed Lee Smith, Trevor Hoffman and John Franco (424).

"You don't envision someone doing what he does for 10 years," manager Joe Torre said. "That's normally not a spot where you have longevity. He's been remarkable, and there's no reason why he can't do it for another four or five years."

In grading performance, teammate Mike Myers noted, "There has to be somebody that's the best or the first to do something. And I think everybody grades down from him. There's nobody that you can grade up to with him.

"Even today, I don't think there's anybody who can say there's somebody better."

When Kyle Farnsworth came up lame in his second frame, Rivera entered with two on, nobody out in the eighth and the Yanks leading by two.

Juan Uribe bunted two balls foul before popping out to second. On the next pitch, Scott Podsednik, 2-for-2 with two walks to that point, nubbed a tailor-made, double-play grounder to second. Rivera exited the eighth after seven pitches.

Tadahito Iguchi hit a wind-blown double to right to start the ninth, and Jim Thome walked. But Rivera jumped ahead on Paul Konerko 0-and-2 and forced a double-play grounder to short. Jermaine Dye ended the game whiffing on 96 mph heat as the Yankees won for the seventh time in eight games to close within a half-game of Boston.

"We did everything we could for perfect baseball," Giambi said. "I think by far, our best three games."

Derek Jeter and Rodriguez tag-teamed Chicago's Freddy Garcia with first-inning homers, and the Yankees led 6-2 by the fourth. When they absolutely needed to drop the hammer, they summoned their cornerstone closer.

"On the field and off the field, he's a Hall of Famer," Chicago manager Ozzie Guillen said. "Young people should look up to him. He's the perfect player. God bless Joe Torre's Mariano." ∎

Mariano Rivera reacts on the round as he closed out the Yankees' 6-4 win over the Chicago White Sox on July 16, 2006. Rivera became just the fourth pitcher to reach 400 career saves. (Getty Images)

Rivera poses with
U.S. Military Academy
cadets at West Point
before the Yankees
took on the Army
baseball team in
an exhibition game
on March 30, 2013.
(N.Y. Post: Charles
Wenzelberg)

Passing a Legend

Mo 2nd All-Time in Saves

September 16, 2008 · By George A. King III

The final week of the old Yankee Stadium was supposed to arrive in October and be ushered in with the red, white and blue banners that are the calling card of big events.

Instead, the last days of the baseball cathedral turned into Milestones, Auditions and Memory Lane.

With the Yankees' playoff chances Kate Moss thin, all that was left for the sold-out crowds to watch was Derek Jeter's climb to the top of the Stadium's all-time hit list, Mariano Rivera moving up on the all-time save chart and to take mental and physical snapshots of the fading ballpark.

"The fans are making it a lot of fun for us," Jeter said after a 4-2 win over the White Sox in front of 53,236. "It's almost like a playoff atmosphere."

Jeter went 0-for-4 and remained tied with Lou Gehrig at 1,269 Stadium hits with six games remaining.

With flashes going off as he attempts to swing, Jeter can't help but notice the attention he is receiving.

"I don't know what to expect," said Jeter, who fanned in the first and third innings, lined into a double play in the fifth and popped up in the seventh. "You see it, but it's mostly on the side so it doesn't affect you."

Rivera, who refuses to bathe in the personal spot-light, recorded the final three outs for his 36th save of the season and the 479th of his career. That vaulted him past Lee Smith into second place on the list. Trevor Hoffman, still active, tops the list with 552.

"It's all right, it's OK," said Rivera, "We won."

As for the auditions, Jeter and Rivera weren't part of that.

However, Alfredo Aceves and Phil Coke used the final month of the season and days of the Stadium to make a case for them moving across the street instead to the minor leagues.

Aceves, who beat the AL West champion Angels a week earlier in Anaheim, allowed two runs and five hits in six innings.

Coke, a 26-year-old lefty who the Pirates refused to take in the Xavier Nady deal because they believed there was a shoulder problem, posted his first big league win with a scoreless seventh inning.

"I am still waiting for it to hit me because I am pretty sure it will be as big as a truck," said Coke.

Jeter and Rivera don't know another big league home than the Stadium. Nor do they understand what a dark October is all about. The latter is as certain to happen as the Stadium closing at season's end.

"The closer we get to Sunday it will sink in that it's the final season," Jeter said. ∎

Mariano Rivera delivers a pitch against the Chicago White Sox on September 15, 2008. Rivera recorded the save that night, the 479th of his career, moving him past Lee Smith into second place on baseball's all-time saves list. (N.Y. Post: Charles Wenzelberg)

Simply THE BEST

In 1999, the Yankee Stadium staff began playing Metallica's "Enter Sandman" when Rivera came into the game. The song stuck, and fans soon began referring to the Yankees closer as "Sandman." Fans at Yankee Stadium during the June 2006 Subway Series between the Yankees and Mets made it clear who they wanted to see on the mound. (N.Y. Post: Charles Wenzelberg)

Mariano's Mountain

Rivera's Remarkable Rise from Poor, Soft-Throwing Non-Prospect to the Apex of Baseball Greatness

September 21, 2011 · By Joel Sherman

Don't start at zero. You will not get the full impact of Mariano Rivera's journey, even if no one in history has ever taken the road from zero to 602 saves before.

To fully appreciate the scope — to understand completely — you must begin at less than zero. You must compute the staggering odds against Rivera throwing even one major league pitch, much less enough to become a legend; the face of October majesty; the greatest late-game weapon in the history of baseball.

You must go back to a fishing village in Panama and milk cartons for gloves. You must go back to a $2,000 signing bonus and an 85 mph fastball. You must go back to non-prospect status and elbow surgery. You must go back to being left unprotected in the expansion draft and nearly being traded for Felix Fermin.

You have to go back to before there was a single save, before anyone had a clue that the skinny kid from Puerto Caimito would throw, arguably, the most distinct pitch the game has ever seen.

For if you think Tom Brady has come far from the sixth round to NFL greatness or Albert Pujols has had an amazing road from Maple Woods Community College and the 13th round to immortality, then know this: Arguably no athlete has ever traveled further to go farther than Rivera.

Go back to Panama in the late 1980s, not exactly a hotbed for baseball. Imagine the dusty fields of the 1989 national tournament and focus on the shortstop with the good arm. See him volunteer to pitch because the ace of the team was doing so poorly.

Watch Mariano Rivera do so well that two

Mariano Rivera delivers a pitch against the Baltimore Orioles on a foggy April 2011 night at Yankee Stadium. (N.Y. Post: Charles Wenzelberg)

of his teammates — Claudino Hernandez and Emilio Gaez — tip off a Yankees scout named Chico Heron, who invites the righty to a tryout camp. Heron likes the looseness in Rivera's arm, likes it so much Rivera is invited to stay for the entire week of the camp.

No other club is interested in Rivera. He is 20, very old for a Latin prospect. His fastball is rudimentary, mainly clocking about 85-87 mph. But the head of the Yankees' Latin operations, Herb Raybourn, has his imagination going. What would that 155-pound kid with all that athleticism look like with some weight on his bones? What could the fastball become then?

So in February 1990, Raybourn travels to Puerto Caimito. This is where the Riveras dance with poverty. This is where Rivera's father — Captain Mariano — operates another man's shrimp boat. This is where a $2,000 signing bonus isn't an insult, like back in the States. So in his father's

Above: A Yankees fan in Anaheim holds up a sign showing support for Rivera during the 2005 ALDS. Opposite: Rivera and teammates celebrate after the closer recorded his 500th career save against the Mets at Citi Field on June 28, 2009. (N.Y. Post: Charles Wenzelberg)

home, Rivera signs his first professional contract. He is off, but certainly not running.

Under the direction of Brian Sabean, now the Giants general manager, the Yankees minor league policy in the early 1990s is to use pitching prospects as either starters or closers. Rivera is neither. He is such an organizational afterthought that he is deployed as a spot starter and a middle reliever even as he puts up good numbers and demonstrates the impeccable control that would become his hallmark.

Wait, the obstacles are not quite large enough yet. Rivera, trying to expand his starter's repertoire, incurs nerve damage by overthrowing breaking balls. Think about that: Two decades ago, Mariano Rivera needed surgery because he couldn't master the art of making a ball break enough. His rehab includes playing catch with Ron Guidry and Whitey Ford, and you can imagine this being as close to greatness as Rivera will get.

He makes just 10 starts in 1992, again pitches very well. But he is only at Single-A. He is turning 23 in November, the same month as the expansion draft to stock the Marlins and Rockies. The Yanks protect pitchers such as Mark Hutton, Domingo Jean and Sam Militello. But they never feel compelled to protect Rivera. Each round they pull three more players back, none is Rivera. And three rounds go by and neither the Marlins nor Rockies select a budding genius.

Instead, Rivera stays a Yankee. His arm gets stronger and — as Herb Raybourn believed — better nutrition and training have added miles per hour on the fastball. By 1995, Rivera has married elite athleticism, a stoic demeanor, unflinching self-confidence and pinpoint precision to be ranked as the Yankees' ninth-best prospect by

Baseball America. But that wasn't even best in his family. His cousin, outfielder Ruben Rivera, was first, followed by Derek Jeter and Andy Pettitte.

Rivera is still a starter midway through the 1995 season when the Yanks contemplate trading him to Detroit for David Wells. But in what Rivera would describe as an act of divinity, his fastball suddenly reaches new heights, climbing to the 95 mph range. Then-general manager Gene Michael refuses to deal him. That October, Michael becomes even more impressed. Nobody in the Yankees bullpen can slow down the Mariners of Ken Griffey Jr. and Edgar Martinez and Jay Buhner. No one but Rivera.

Used more out of desperation than inspiration by manager Buck Showalter, Rivera throws 5⅓ shutout innings in the Division Series. The Yanks lose anyway.

Still, this is Rivera's route, which means nothing simple, nothing handed to him. So he begins next spring with a new manager in Joe Torre, but a familiar role, which is to say none. The organization, meanwhile, is fretting about trying to win with a rookie shortstop named Jeter. And here are the Mariners breaking in their own young shortstop, Alex Rodriguez, and suddenly Fermin is available. Seattle asks for either Rivera or Bob Wickman.

The Yanks' top brass meets the week before the 1996 season begins. They decide to stick with the rookie shortstop, evading perhaps the worst day in organization history: Trading Rivera and demoting Jeter.

Instead, Rivera and Jeter, who had played together at four different stops in the minors, become breakout stars for the 1996 champions, cornerstones of a dynasty. Rivera is a long man in April 1996 and indispensable by May. Torre recognizes the weapon. The ball is flying out of ballparks like never before, but no one can hit the skinny

Sporting a throwback uniform on the 100th anniversary of Fenway Park, Rivera delivers a pitch against the Red Sox on April 20, 2012. (N.Y. Post: Charles Wenzelberg)

righty. Rivera finally has a role. Well, actually many roles. To this team he is middleman and set-up man, lefty specialist and righty specialist.

And on May 17, 1996 — with closer John Wetteland unavailable — Rivera pitches the ninth to protect an 8-5 victory over the Angels. Career save No. 1. He is already 26 years old, still a season away from replacing Wetteland as the full-time closer. He has yet to perfect the pitch that will define him: A cut fastball that will snap bats and break hearts.

Yet here he is now, at 41, the all-time save king and, perhaps, the greatest postseason pitcher ever. He has more saves than the next three men on the Yankee all-time list — Dave Righetti, Goose Gossage and Sparky Lyle — combined. He is a testament to durability; the only man to pitch in more than 1,000 games for just one team and the last man who will have the honor of wearing No. 42 in the majors.

He has never won a Cy Young or the MVP, but nobody has pitched better than him over the last 15 years and no one has been more valuable to his team winning. He has used steely self-belief, flawless mechanics and an imperturbable nature to dominate an era. Rivera has created an indomitable dichotomy: His pitches break late and viciously, yet obey his commands. So he has walked few, limited homers and dominated lefties — a three-part formula at the center of his brilliance.

It seems incredible to think that he was unsigned until 20, not even considered much of a prospect until 24. The path from where he started to where he is today feels as though implausible married impossible. But this is no fairy tale. This was earned with sweat, strength and savvy. The all-time save king is a champion of durability and dependability, of confidence and conditioning, of inner strength and utter conviction.

Mariano Rivera's excursion to all-time save king began at less than zero. And we still don't know where it ends. ■

In a rare show of emotion on the mound, Rivera celebrates with teammates after breaking Trevor Hoffman's career saves record on September 19, 2011. (N.Y. Post: Charles Wenzelberg)

The House That Mo Closed

Rivera, Pettitte Give Stadium Winning Sendoff

September 22, 2008 · By Mike Puma

The House That Mo Closed officially belongs to the history books.

In the only acceptable conclusion for the ghosts of Ruth, Gehrig, DiMaggio and Mantle, the Yankees said farewell to the Stadium with one last memorable performance.

Adhering to the script, that meant a couple of home runs, favorite son Andy Pettitte getting the win and Mariano Rivera on the mound to record the final out of a 7-3 victory over the Orioles.

"It's important that this building goes out the way it's viewed upon, as a winning building," said Joe Girardi, whose Yankees won for the eighth time in nine games to keep their playoff hopes tethered to dental floss.

With Boston's victory over Toronto earlier in the day, the Yanks' Tragic Number for elimination from the playoff race was reduced to 1.

For the Yankees, the night had Game 7 of the World Series intensity on multiple levels.

"This might have been the most nervous you can be going into a game," Johnny Damon said. "We knew this was a must-win and going down two runs early we needed a big hit and I was able to get one."

But though Damon's three-run homer in the third inning against Chris Waters (3-4) was big, it likely will be forgotten because of Jose Molina's shot an inning later.

Molina became the answer to a trivia question by drilling a two-run homer into the netting behind the left-field fence that gave the Yanks a 5-3 lead. Babe Ruth hit the first home run in the Stadium's history on April 18, 1923 and Molina the last on Sept. 21, 2008.

Pettitte pitched five-plus innings and allowed three earned runs on seven hits with one walk and three strikeouts. The lefthander, unsigned beyond this season, has battled recent arm soreness and isn't a lock to make his final scheduled start on Saturday in Boston.

Adam Jones singled leading off the sixth, prompting Girardi to summon Jose Veras. Pettitte departed to a huge standing ovation and was clearly wiping away tears as he walked to the dugout, from which he made a curtain call.

"It almost felt like a playoff series we just won," Pettitte said. "How tired I am right now, emotionally tired....it's just weird." ∎

The Yankees hosted the All-Star Game during the final season at old Yankee Stadium in 2008. Rivera poses with singer Sheryl Crow before the game. (N.Y. Post: Charles Wenzelberg)

500 Saves, 1 of a Kind

Peerless Rivera Reaches Milestone, Clinches Sweep

June 29, 2009 · By Joel Sherman

Five hundred saves earlier Mariano Rivera was a skinny novice who did not yet have the pitch that would make him immortal or the theme song that would become his entrance trademark.

Back in 1996, throwing mainly to the man who is now his manager, Rivera relied almost exclusively on a placid delivery that lulled hitters before — boom! — menacing four-seam fastballs whooshed by at the top of the strike zone.

He began that season as the last pitcher on the staff, but was so quickly effective that then-manager Joe Torre kept expanding and expanding his role, from mop-up, to long relief, to setup and — on May 17, 1996 — to closer when John Wetteland was sidelined with an injury.

Rivera finished off the Angels in the ninth that day, inducing Garret Anderson to ground out into a game-ending double play. It was the first of his 230 saves at the old Yankee Stadium, the first in a career of genius.

No. 500 came and, perhaps just as memorably, so did his first career RBI. That the RBI came against Francisco Rodriguez brought a final humiliating touch to a three-game Yankees sweep in the Mets' home: Rivera drawing a bases-loaded walk to deliver an insurance run for himself in a 4-2 Yankees triumph.

Citi Field represented the 27th different stadium in which Rivera registered a save. His first came with manager Joe Girardi catching him and No. 500 came with Girardi summoning him to clean up Brian Bruney's eighth-inning mess: Two on, two out, Yankees up just 3-2.

On the road, there was no "Enter Sandman" upon his arrival. But there was his signature pitch. Rivera developed his cutter once he became a full-time closer. It took him to save No. 500. It will take him to Cooperstown.

The Yankees honored Mariano Rivera's 500 career saves, presenting him with a ring at a ceremony at Yankee Stadium on September 29, 2009. Rivera's son, Jafet, hugged his father as Mariano accepted the ring. (N.Y. Post: Charles Wenzelberg)

The count moved full on Omir Santos, and Rivera fired a 92-mile-per-hour cutter that inched from off the plate to the inside corner. Another precision strike three. Another crisis averted. The first step toward what would be the 110th save of Rivera's career that required more than three outs.

Rivera returned to the bench for familiar rest. But that was interrupted. The Mets decided to intentionally walk Derek Jeter with two outs to load the bases because it brought up Rivera for just the third at-bat of his career. The drama intensified as the count moved full, and then Rivera took an inside fastball for ball four. The Yankees bench rose in joy.

When the All-Star Game was at Yankee Stadium in 2008, Rivera ordered the clubhouse attendants to keep K-Rod's locker away from his because he did not particularly like Rodriguez's on-field theatrics.

Rivera then went back to the mound to do what he does best: throw one fastball after another toward triumph. He induced Luis Castillo to ground out and struck out Jeremy Reed before Daniel Murphy dropped a soft single to left. Alex Cora came up as the tying run.

"No chance," Rivera said when asked before the game if he ever imagined getting to 500.

But Cora swung at the first pitch, another easy grounder. Robinson Cano fielded and tossed to first. Save 500 was in the books. Only Rivera and Trevor Hoffman have reached that total.

Yankees teammates surrounded and hugged their most respected teammate. As usual there was not a ton of emotion from Rivera. He had done this 500 times in the regular season and been the key figure in a dynasty. There was a broad smile. That was his celebration. ∎

With his family looking on, Mariano Rivera's son Jaziel accepts a ring from Yankees manager Joe Girardi during the September 29, 2009, ceremony at Yankee Stadium commemorating Rivera's 500th career save. (N.Y. Post: Charles Wenzelberg)

One Mo Time

Even Reggie Says Rivera is Bombers' True "Mr. October"

November 3, 2009 · By Mike Puma

Alex Rodriguez made the biggest splash in fall 2009 for the Yankees, but it was Mariano Rivera who seemed like the team's postseason MVP as Game 5 of the World Series approached.

Rivera isn't permitted to have a bad game at this time of year, and he hadn't. He entered with five saves and a 0.63 ERA on the postseason, a big reason the Yankees were within 27 outs of world championship No. 27.

A night earlier, Phillies closer Brad Lidge entered a tie game in the ninth inning and surrendered three runs in the Yankees' 7-4 victory. That added Lidge to the list of closers — the Twins' Joe Nathan and the Angels' Brian Fuentes are the others — who stumbled in a big spot against the Yankees that postseason.

Rivera's closest brush with mortality was allowing a run against the Angels in Game 6 of the AL Championship Series.

"I don't think there are words that can describe how good he's been, not only this year, but the 40 years he's been playing, it feels like," Joba Chamberlain said. "Every time I turn on the TV in the postseason, it feels like I watch Mo get an out."

Reggie Jackson has suggested that Rivera is the Yankees' true Mr. October, and it would be difficult to argue with the player who first made the moniker famous.

Rivera recorded his 11th career World Series save in Game 4 — extending his own record — and moved ahead of Whitey Ford by appearing in his 23rd career World Series game.

The Phillies' Game 6 starter, Cliff Lee (0.54 ERA) entered as the only pitcher with a minimum of 30 innings pitched sporting a better career postseason earned run average than Rivera's 0.75.

"It's been a blessing," Yankees general manager Brian Cashman said. "[Rivera] is a guy that we gave very little money to out of a small fishing village in Panama, and he's moved to the biggest city in the world it seems like and became the greatest of all time at what he does. It's a great story in itself, and we've been blessed to have him here doing what he's doing as long as he's done it."

Rivera was on the mound to record the final out of the Yankees' three straight world championships from 1998-2000 and was hoping last night to again throw the final pitch of the season. Rivera earned his first championship ring setting up closer John Wetteland in 1996.

Rivera holds up a copy of the *New York Post* following the Yankees' Game 6 win over the Philadelphia Phillies to clinch the 2009 World Series, the team's 27th championship. (N.Y. Post: Charles Wenzelberg)

Manager Joe Girardi said the argument could be made that Rivera is the greatest postseason player ever.

"I don't look at everyone's numbers and what everyone has done in the postseason, but Mo has been as good as anyone," Girardi said. "He has dominated."

Chamberlain, who shifted to the bullpen after spending the regular season starting, said he has enjoyed getting reacquainted with Rivera.

"Just to sit in the bullpen and watch him and talk to him [you] realize why he's so good," Chamberlain said. "He pays attention to every small detail, to the way a guy stands in the box to the way he does things early in the game.

"Sometimes it gets intimidating to talk to him, but he makes it so easy for us to approach him and ask him any question that is on our mind or how to get a guy out." ∎

Above: Longtime Yankees teammates Rivera, Derek Jeter (center) and Andy Pettitte (right) celebrate after winning the 2009 World Series. It was the Yankees' first title since 2000. Opposite: Jeter and Rivera savor a moment with the Commissioner's Trophy after the Yankees' Game 6 win. (N.Y. Post: Charles Wenzelberg)

Mo-Mentous

Rivera Blows Away M's for 600th Save

September 14, 2011 · By George A. King III

Given a choice between the five World Series rings he owns and breaking Trevor Hoffman's saves record, Mariano Rivera said it's not much of a choice.

"Nothing compares to the World Series," Rivera said after his 600th career save sealed a 3-2 Yankees victory over the Mariners in front of an announced crowd of 18,306 at Safeco Field. "I [like] the World Series better."

Rivera stood one save away from tying Hoffman for the all-time saves mark and two from standing alone at the top of the list. Not one to dwell on individual accomplishments, Rivera said 602 would be significant.

"Don't get me wrong, [600] is a great number," said Rivera, who watched Russell Martin throw out Ichiro Suzuki attempting to swipe second base for the final out. "The next one [601] is the big one."

Rivera's 41st save in 46 chances on the year made a winner out of A.J. Burnett for the first time since Aug. 15.

After struggling through the first three innings, Burnett made an adjustment with his hips to add more turn to his delivery and was impressive in the final three frames.

"The ball wasn't coming out good and I wasn't comfortable," said Burnett, who kept his hands higher, as he had done in his previous three starts.

In six innings, Burnett gave up two runs, four hits, hit two, hiked his MLB-leading wild pitch count to 25 and fanned a season-high 11.

Rivera gave up a one-out single to Suzuki in the ninth, struck out Kyle Seager swinging for the second out and watched Martin grab an inside pitch and nail Suzuki.

"I didn't realize it until I saw guys on the mound," Martin said of Rivera notching the 600th save.

Rivera vanished in a crowd of teammates after the final out and shared an embrace with Derek Jeter, whose 3,000th hit earlier in the season gave the Yankees two awe-inspiring milestones.

"I'm not surprised by it. I've been playing with him since I was 18 years old," said Jeter, who stretched his hit streak to 12 games with a leadoff single. "I said, 'Congratulations.' I know how important it is to him to do his job. He takes pride in the job."

Rafael Soriano worked a spotless seventh inning and David Robertson left the bases loaded in the eighth and turned a one-run lead over to Rivera.

Robinson Cano homered in a two-run second and drove in the third run with a fielder's choice ground ball.

When Rivera was done getting mobbed on the mound, Jorge Posada and Burnett were waiting in the clubhouse. Posada showered Rivera with champagne and Burnett smothered Rivera's face with shaving cream.

"I don't know if we will ever see [again] what Mo and Trevor Hoffman have done," Girardi said. "He is the best closer ever in the game. He has given Yankee fans something to be proud of." ∎

Rivera delivers a pitch against the Seattle Mariners at Safeco Field on September 13, 2011. He recorded his 600th career save in the Yankees' win, just two saves short of breaking Trevor Hoffman's major league record. (Getty Images)

Sultan of Save

Rivera is No. 1 With Save 602

September 20, 2011 · By Mark Hale

Alone in history. Alone on the mound. After Mariano Rivera became baseball's all-time saves leader with No. 602 in The Bronx, zipping through three Twins in the Yankees' 6-4 win, teammates Jorge Posada and Alex Rodriguez convinced the closer not to leave the mound.

Rivera stayed put and took a celebratory curtain call as the Yankee Stadium crowd saluted the 41-year-old franchise legend's record-breaking feat. He waved to the fans and tipped his cap in appreciation.

"I think it was his moment," Posada said. "So we needed him to stay on the mound and reflect on a great career."

"Great" does not adequately describe it. Rivera, a future first-ballot Hall of Famer, is the most sublime closer in baseball history, and he made it official when he broke his all-time saves tie with Trevor Hoffman, earning his 602nd 15 years and 125 days after his first (May 17, 1996) and two days after his 601st.

"It feels great," Rivera said, flanked at his press conference by sons Mariano Jr., Jafet and Jaziel. "Don't get me wrong, it feels good. I wasn't expecting it. But thank God it happened. Thank God it's over too, because I was getting a little uncomfortable with all this [attention]."

The Yankees held a 6-4 lead from the sixth inning on, and with the knowledge that a cushion of four runs or more would remove the save situation, the fans roared when Nick Swisher ended the bottom of the eighth by grounding into a double play.

"I didn't think I'd ever hear the day where people would cheer for us to make outs," manager Joe Girardi said.

Soon enough, Metallica's "Enter Sandman" began playing, and the ovation came as Rivera jogged in from the bullpen.

Rivera needed just 13 pitches for a 1-2-3 ninth, retiring Trevor Plouffe on a groundout to second, taking care of Michael Cuddyer on a fly ball to right and catching Chris Parmelee looking at a called strike three.

Rivera's teammates surrounded him in front of the mound and hugged him while the scoreboard displayed, "ALLTIME CAREER SAVES LEADER."

"For the first time in my career, I'm on the mound alone," Rivera said. "I can't describe that feeling. Because it was priceless."

Posada said the Yankees had not planned to have Rivera remain on the mound for the salute.

"It just came up in my head," said Posada, a teammate since both players debuted in 1995. "I said, 'Stay on the mound a little bit longer.'"

He would turn 42 after the season.

"It's remarkable at his age that he's still doing it at this level," said Girardi, whose team lowered its magic number to 4 to clinch a playoff spot and 5 to clinch the AL East.

"Mo's special, man," Posada said. "His heart is humongous." ∎

A multiple-exposure view of Mariano Rivera delivering the final pitch to Minnesota's Chris Parmelee — a called strike three — as Rivera completed his 602nd career save, passing Trevor Hoffman for the No. 1 spot on the all-time list. (N.Y. Post: Charles Wenzelberg)

No Mo!

Rivera Tears ACL Shagging Fly Balls Before Game

May 4, 2012 · By George A. King III

The last image of Mariano Rivera on the field in a Yankees uniform in 2012 had him writhing in pain on the warning track of Kauffman Stadium.

Diagnosed by Dr. Vincent Key, the Royals team physician, with a torn ACL in his right knee, the best closer of all time said he also had a meniscus issue after undergoing an MRI.

"At this point I don't know," a damp-eyed Rivera answered when asked if he would pitch again. "We have to fight this first."

The Yankees said the torn ACL was a preliminary diagnosis but one look around a somber clubhouse told a different story.

Alex Rodriguez, who witnessed Rivera stumbling on the track when his cleats skidded on the dirt while shagging a Jayson Nix batting practice fly ball, had a hard time talking about it.

But as Rodriguez stood near home plate awaiting his swings during batting practice and saw his teammate crumple, he yelled, "Oh, my God! Oh, my God!"

"It's bad, there is no other way to put it," said Derek Jeter, whose four hits weren't enough for the Yankees to avoid a 4-3 loss to the Royals.

"Mo is a vital part of the team. You don't replace him. Other guys have to pick it up."

Rivera, who walked with a heavy limp in the clubhouse, said he will stay with the club before being examined by Yankees' physician Chris Ahmad in New York.

However, he knows surgery awaits.

"The ACL is torn and some meniscus, too," Rivera said. "I didn't think it was that bad but it's torn and I have to fix it."

"If that's what it is, it's as bad as it gets," Girardi said of the diagnosis.

Since the career-threatening injury occurred while Rivera was shagging balls during batting practice, some will question why a 42-year-old pitcher would be doing that.

However, nobody inside the Yankees' organization was taking that approach. Especially Rivera.

"I don't want it any other way. I was doing what I love to do, shagging I love to do," said Rivera, who uses the activity to keep his legs strong and his mind at ease. "If I had to do it over again I would do it."

Since Rivera strongly hinted in spring training that 2012 was going to be his final

Mariano Rivera is carted off the Kauffman Stadium field after injuring his knee while shagging fly balls during batting practice on May 3, 2012. The injury sidelined Rivera for the remainder of the season. (AP Images)

season and that ACL surgery often takes six to eight months to recover from, there's a possibility Rivera is finished.

"I told you before the game that this game is cruel," Mark Teixeira said. "It's even more cruel. This is terrible."

Rivera's presence in the clubhouse is huge. On the mound, well, there aren't enough adjectives to describe what he has meant to the Yankees since taking over the closer's role in 1997.

"I have always argued that he is the best pitcher of all time, not a reliever, the best pitcher of all time," Teixeira said of Rivera, who tops the all-time list.

The pain in the knee wasn't as bad as what was going in Rivera's head.

"I let the team down," said Rivera, who was on the verge of tears. ∎

Above:: Rivera grimaces in pain while being attended to after injuring his right knee. Opposite: Yankees manager Joe Girardi helps the injured Rivera off the field. (AP Images)

Rivera Vows Return

ACL Tear Won't Stop Legend

May 5, 2012 · By George A. King III and Ken Davidoff

Mariano Rivera didn't want a brilliant career to end on a dirt warning track at Kauffman Stadium.

One day after suffering a torn ACL and meniscus damage to his right knee shagging batting practice fly balls, the game's all-time saves leader announced his career wasn't over and that he would attempt a comeback for the 2013 season.

"I am coming back. Put it down," Rivera said. "Write it down. In big letters."

With a wide smile, and joking around with reporters, Rivera sat in front of his locker before the Yankees' 6-2 win over the Royals and said he made the decision overnight in his hotel room.

"When you love the game and you like to compete, it would be tough to go out like this," he said. "I can't go down like this."

Rivera said, prior to the injury, he hadn't fully decided to retire after this season. He was thinking that through, he said, "but now, everything is out the window."

Rivera, 42, would be a free agent after this year. He expressed confidence the Yankees would want him back.

"Oh, yeah. They will want the old goat," he said.

Before the game, Rivera addressed his teammates.

"He said, 'Don't change anything and don't feel sorry for me,'" Robertson said. "'I am going to come back.'" That jibed with what Rivera told reporters he was going to do.

"I'm just going to give them encouragement that I trust them and believe in them," he said. "They can do the job. They will do the job."

Joe Girardi said he would use Rafael Soriano and Robertson in closing roles depending on the workload of each right-hander.

The news Rivera planned on coming back in 2013 was met with anticipation.

The day after Rivera sustained a devastating knee injury, a Yankees fan at Kansas City's Kauffman Stadium holds up a sign wishing Rivera well in his recovery. (N.Y. Post: Charles Wenzelberg)

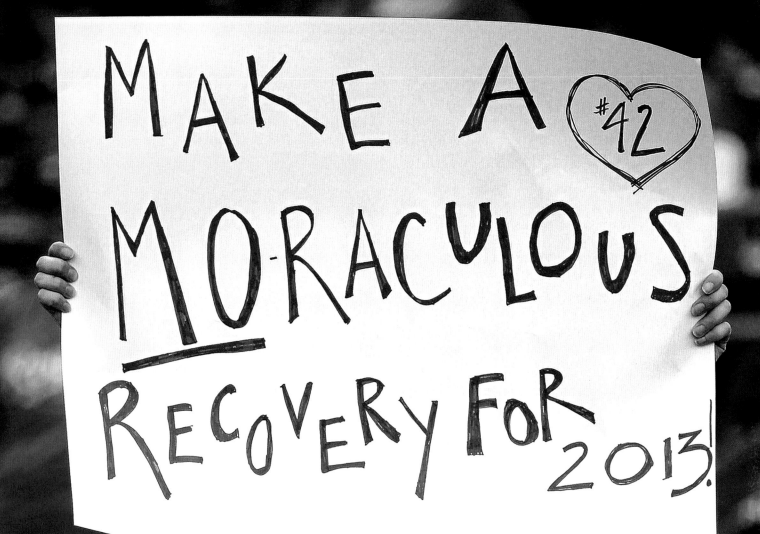

"When you love the game and you like to compete, it would be tough to go out like this. I can't go down like this."

—Mariano Rivera

"It's great news," said Alex Rodriguez. "It's surprising, very. It's super, for me selfishly because I love Mo and for the organization. I have never seen a guy who does so good at what he does."

Mark Teixeira said he wasn't convinced Rivera was going to retire after the season before the injury.

"I was thinking he was coming back anyway, I didn't believe he was going to retire," Teixeira said. "He is still one of the best players in the game. It's great to hear and it will be good for his rehab, something for him to look forward to."

Derek Jeter was happy to hear the news that Rivera will try to return, but stressed there are almost five months left in this season.

"Everyone is happy to hear that, but we can't sit around and wait," the captain said. "Injuries are unfortunate. Injuries happen. But we still have work to do and jobs to do. We can't count the days." ∎

Rivera kept busy after his 2012 season ended prematurely. The Yankees closer rang the bell to open the New York Stock Exchange on July 18, 2012. (AP Images)

Closer to the End

With "Tank Almost Empty," Closer Makes Final Season Official

March 10, 2013 · By George A. King III

Mariano Rivera checked the gas gauge, saw the needle near empty and decided a marvelous journey will end whenever the final out of the coming season is logged.

"Now is the time. The tank is almost empty," Rivera said when he announced the 2013 season would be the end of an 18-year career that will never be matched. "The little gas that I have left is for this year. There is nothing left. I did everything and I am proud of it."

Rivera admitted if he hadn't torn the ACL in his right knee the previous May, 2012 would have been it for the game's all-time saves leader. However, he wasn't going to sign off on a Hall of Fame career by being carted out of Kansas City's Kauffman Stadium.

"I don't want to leave home, I want to stay home," Rivera said. "But I know I have a job to do and I am here to do the best."

Rivera said his desire to compete hasn't evaporated, but time away from his family led to his decision that, he said, was made before spring training opened.

"I will never stop missing the game, the action and the field," Rivera said. "The traveling and the hotels, I say, 'No more.'"

Rivera's press conference was attended by every Yankees uniform in camp, general partner Hal Steinbrenner, executive vice president Felix Lopez, general manager Brian Cashman and assistant GM Jean Afterman.

All got a chuckle out of Rivera starting the press conference by jokingly thanking Cashman for a two-year contract extension. Rivera said he was moved that every player in camp attended his announcement.

With Andy Pettitte, who tried retirement for one season and came back to pitch, sitting nearby, Rivera was asked about the possibility he could change his mind.

"I have few bullets left and I am going to use them this year," said Rivera, who will start his final season with 608 regular-season saves and a record 42 in the postseason. "I know after

After announcing that the 2013 season would be his last, Mariano Rivera ran out onto the field to join his teammates at the Yankees' spring training complex. (N.Y. Post: Charles Wenzelberg)

this year you won't see me on the field unless I am doing something else than playing baseball.

"It's not in me anymore. I did what I love. I did it with passion, but after this year I won't do it for the wrong reasons. I don't want to do it for money or traveling. I want to close the door and do what's next."

Rivera said he has an interest in staying close to the game by tutoring minor league players and said he doesn't agree he is the best ever to close.

"I don't feel that I am the greatest of all time," he said. "I am a team player, and if it wasn't for my teammates I never would have had the opportunity. I would love to be remembered as a player who was always there for others, trying to make others better. That is the legacy I want to leave, that I was there for others."

Since 1996, Rivera has been there for the Yankees, their closer since 1997. And to think George Steinbrenner had to be talked out of trading Rivera to Seattle for shortstop Felix Fermin in 1996 because The Boss was being told Derek Jeter wasn't ready for the big leagues.

Jeter certainly has had much to do with the Yankees winning five World Series in the last 16 years. Yet the Yankees' MVP across those seasons has been Rivera.

Now, the end is upon him and Rivera knows the way he wants to exit.

"The last game I hope is the last pitch of the World Series," Rivera said. "That is how I envision my last game." ∎

With his teammates looking on, Mariano Rivera announced on March 9, 2013, that he would be retiring after the upcoming season. (N.Y. Post: Charles Wenzelberg)

Dynamic Duo Cures Woes

Pettitte, Rivera Lead Yankees to First 2013 Win

April 5, 2013 · By Ken Davidoff

The Yankees and their fans had a fever, to borrow from Christopher Walken in the classic "Saturday Night Live" sketch. And the only prescription? Pettitte and Rivera.

Victory number one for these 2013 Yankees, a much-needed, 4-2 defeat of the Red Sox at a very chilly Yankee Stadium, came courtesy of their two oldest players. The two most tenured active employees in pinstripes.

While Derek Jeter slowly rehabilitates his left ankle down in Tampa, his fellow quintuple World Series champions restored some order to The Bronx before the Yankees departed for Detroit. And you wonder, for about the 1,000th time in 19 years, where exactly the Yankees would be without the outstanding duo of 40-year-old Andy Pettitte and 43-year-old Mariano Rivera.

"I'm glad I could contribute, obviously, and give us a good outing," Pettitte said, in a cheery Yankees clubhouse. "Obviously, I feel real, real good and secure about things whenever I see that guy running in from the bullpen in the ninth inning."

"I always want to save the game. Not only for him, but for everybody else," Rivera said. "But at the same time, it's special when Andy goes there and does the kind of job he knows how to do and allows me to close the game for him."

Pettitte did the heavy lifting, as starting pitchers usually do, throwing eight masterful innings in his first start of the season. He needed just 94 pitches to give the Yankees' non-closers a night off in the bullpen, inducing the Red Sox to hit into three double plays. Masterful.

Then came the night's top drama. For the first time since April 30 of 2012, "Enter Sandman" filled up The Stadium, and Rivera kicked off his final campaign with a shaky, one-run save, the 609th of his career, concluding the game by getting rookie Jackie Bradley Jr. to look at an 89-mph cutter for strike three. Thus Rivera completed his comeback from the season-ending surgery on his right knee, from a torn ACL he suffered May 3 in Kansas City.

"It was wonderful," Rivera said. "You wait for almost a year to be on the mound and get your job done. Especially here at home."

It marked the 69th time in the regular season

Mariano Rivera and teammates celebrate the Yankees' 4-2 win over the Boston Red Sox on April 4, 2013, at Yankee Stadium. Rivera saved the game for Andy Pettitte, his first save since sustaining a serious knee injury in May 2012. (Getty Images)

that Pettitte and Rivera teamed for a win and save, and their first such effort since July 8, 2010 over the Mariners in Seattle — five days before George Steinbrenner died. They subsequently teamed up to beat the Twins in Game 2 of the 2010 American League Division Series.

The Yankees entered the game teetering as much as a club can teeter two games into a baseball season. Their opener Monday and Game 2 Wednesday had been distinguished by bad offense, bad weather and bad luck against their historic rivals. With fan anxiety at DEFCON 2, the Stadium had emptied out precipitously by the final innings in both contests.

This time, Pettitte kept many of the 40,611 fans captivated, and they surely stuck around as it became increasingly clear they would bear witness to Rivera's triumphant return, as well as the Red Sox's first loss of the season.

Pettitte received a little help in the first inning from an overzealous Shane Victorino, who tried to score from second base on a wild pitch when Pettitte neglected to cover home — Francisco Cervelli gathered his bearings in time to dive, block the plate and tag out Victorino — but after that, it was the classic left-hander.

With his fastball topping at a respectable 90 miles per hour, with his changeup and slider working well, he limited the Red Sox to no hits in their three at-bats with runners in scoring position.

Rivera admitted that he needed a batter to settle in. It's very out of character for him to walk the leadoff batter, as he did Dustin Pedroia. Jonny Gomes' one-out double led to Pedroia coming home on Middlebrooks' grounder to the right side — Rivera covered first, easily — and then came the game-ending strikeout, and the brief celebration.

Rivera, usually reserved, admitted that he doubted, at times, whether he'd make it to this day.

"There were times because of the therapy and the pain and all of that stuff, I was wondering if it would be worth it to come back. You know what I mean?" he said. "But at the same time, the passion and drive that you have for the game motivated me to keep going." ∎

Rivera picked up where he left off in 2013. Here he high-fives with teammates after closing out the Yankees 4-3 win over the Cleveland Indians on June 4. (N.Y. Post: Charles Wenzelberg)

Surreal Entry for Sandman

Rivera Gets Standing Ovation, Pitches Perfect Eighth in Final All-Star Game

July 17, 2013 · By Mike Puma

Mariano Rivera got a hero's welcome on enemy turf and made his final All-Star appearance a Sandman Special.

Summoned in the eighth inning of the 84th All-Star game because manager Jim Leyland wanted to ensure Rivera would get to pitch, the Yankees icon was perfect — and named the Most Valuable Player of the AL's 3-0 domination of the NL before 45,186, the largest crowd in Citi Field history.

"As a team player you don't look for these things, they just happen," said Rivera, who became the first Yankees player since Derek Jeter in 2000 to win the All-Star game MVP award. "I'm honored and proud to be a member of the New York Yankees and being able to play for this city and to do it the way I have done."

Rivera entered to a standing ovation and waved his cap to the crowd upon reaching the mound. To let Rivera bask in the moment, his AL teammates delayed in taking their positions, leaving the future Hall of Fame closer alone during the 60-second ovation.

"It felt so weird — basically I was there alone with my catcher," Rivera said. "I definitely appreciated what they did for me."

Then, Rivera retired the side in order and departed to more applause.

Leyland said it would have been too risky waiting until the ninth to let Rivera pitch. If the NL rallied and took the lead in the eighth, there might not have been a bottom of the ninth.

"You know, I'm probably not the most popular manager in baseball," Leyland said. "I wanted to make sure I got out of here alive tonight."

Rivera's AL teammates also seemed moved by the events.

"I had goose bumps the whole time," Dustin Pedroia said. "It was nice not to worry about facing him." ∎

Mariano Rivera smiles with the 2013 All-Star Game MVP trophy. He pitched a perfect eighth inning as the American League won the game 3-0 at Citi Field. (N.Y. Post: Charles Wenzelberg)

citi FI
LET'S GO
LTA
ORIGINAL
IMPORTED FROM MEXICO
CHOLULA
HOT SAUCE
ORIGINAL
ALL-STAR GAME
20 13
TONIGHT'S MVP
MARIANO
RIVERA
CHEVROLET
1 2 3 4 5 6 7 8
AMERICAN 0 0 0 1 1 0 0 1
NATIONAL 0 0 0 0 0 0 0 0

The Citi Field scoreboard honored Mariano Rivera, who was named the MVP of the 2013 All-Star Game, the first relief pitcher to receive that honor. Rivera was named to 13 All-Star teams in his career. (N.Y. Post: Charles Wenzelberg)

Passing Stars

Rivera's Exit, Harvey's Start Highlight All-Star Game at Citi Field

July 17, 2013 · By Kevin Kernan

Matt Harvey opened the All-Star Game. Mariano Rivera came on in the eighth inning, not his usual ninth, and was named MVP.

The Great Rivera became the first reliever ever to be named MVP of the All-Star Game. The Mets' Harvey, 24, is in his first full season. Rivera, 43, is in his last season with the Yankees.

This was the perfect intersection of two eras in this New York City Midsummer Classic as the American League shut out the National League, 3-0, at Citi Field.

When Rivera signed with the Yankees back in 1990, Harvey was all of 10 months old.

When Rivera entered the game to start the eighth he was given a long standing ovation by the 45,186 fans, the largest crowd in Citi Field history.

He also was alone. His teammates stayed off the field so he could bask in the moment on the mound. It was the ultimate sign of respect. Rivera was given a standing ovation by every other All-Star in the ballpark, too.

Then, when he retired the NL in order in the eighth on 16 pitches, 11 strikes, he was given another standing ovation. As he slowly walked off the field, Tigers ace Justin Verlander was the first to greet him outside the third base dugout.

Rivera said he was incredibly touched by the reception he received from the crowd, but also from the other All-Stars.

"It almost made me cry," Rivera said. "It was beautiful. I have no words to explain it and the appreciation shown to me. I can't describe it. To me it was powerful, knowing the best of the best were standing in front of their dugouts and cheering for me, it means a lot to me. All I can say is thank you."

Rivera was not given the chance to pitch the ninth because AL manager Jim Leyland did not want to take the chance of having the NL take the lead in the bottom of the eighth, not allowing Rivera to pitch in the ninth.

"I wanted to pitch the ninth, but I also wanted to pitch," Rivera said. "If something

Rivera walks off the field with Royals catcher Salvador Perez after pitching a perfect eighth inning in his final All-Star Game appearance. (N.Y. Post: Charles Wenzelberg)

Trout on a fastball away on the first pitch and now he had to face Cabrera with runners on first and second.

"That was when I knew I was going to have to buckle down and obviously the last thing I want to do is get down 3–0 and no outs in an All-Star Game," Harvey said.

The next three AL batters had a combined 87 home runs this season. It could have been 3-0 in a flash. Harvey buckled down, striking out Cabrera on a nasty slider, getting Chris Davis to fly to center and whiffed Jose Bautista.

Harvey didn't hit 100 mph, but he was impressive. In a 1-2-3 second inning, he struck out Baltimore's Adam Jones with a vicious up-and-in 98 mph fastball.

This was a day and night of memories for Harvey, who was the star of the red carpet parade. When he was asked what the highlight of his day was, he made a joke about his bright orange cleats.

"Well, I hope it's not the cleats that I was wearing," he said. "No, just meeting everybody, being in the locker room, playing this game with David [Wright], that was the biggest thing. I think as a kid, you dream of sitting on the side as the Home Run Derby is going on, and that was an awesome event, too. The support that was given in the red carpet [parade], that was indescribable. This whole experience has just been, you know, breathtaking."

Yes, it was in so many ways on this hot mid-summer night in the city. ■

Mariano Rivera tips his cap to the Citi Field crowd after receiving a standing ovation upon entering the game in the eighth inning. (N.Y. Post: Charles Wenzelberg)

The Tampa Bay Rays erected a huge sculpture of Mariano Rivera's head amidst the New York skyline at Tropicana Field. Rivera posed with the sculpture and signed it before the Yankees' August 23, 2013, game against the Rays. (AP Images)

New York City Fire Commissioner Salvatore Cassano (left) and Mets Chief Operating Officer Jeff Wilpon present Mariano Rivera with a fire call box and fire hose nozzle prior to an interleague game between the Yankees and Mets at Citi Field on May 28, 2013. (AP Images)

Twins manager Ron Gardenhire (center) and first baseman Justin Morneau (right) present Mariano Rivera with a rocking chair made of broken bats, called the Chair of Broken Dreams, prior to the Twins-Yankees game at Target Field on July 3, 2013. (AP Images)